WHAT NOW?

HOW TO MOVE INTO YOUR NEXT SEASON

MARK JOBE

MOODY PUBLISHERS
CHICAGO

To the survivors of the COVID-19 pandemic
and anyone in the middle of transition

Edited by Connor Sterchi
Interior Design: Erik M. Peterson
Cover Design: Kelsey Fehlberg

Library of Congress Control Number: 2020939533

ISBN: 978-0-8024-2341-2

Originally delivered by fleets of horse-drawn wagons, the affordable paperbacks from D. L. Moody's publishing house resourced the church and served everyday people. Now, after more than 125 years of publishing and ministry, Moody Publishers' mission remains the same—even if our delivery systems have changed a bit. For more information on other books (and resources) created from a biblical perspective, go to: www.moodypublishers.com or write to:

Moody Publishers
820 N. LaSalle Boulevard
Chicago, IL 60610

1 3 5 7 9 10 8 6 4 2

Printed in the United States of America

CONTENTS

INTRODUCTION

As I sit here writing this introduction, our world has been rocked by a global pandemic and an economic crisis that has plunged millions into an uncertain future. Many are asking what life will look like after the crisis. What will this next season of my life mean to me? When you have been living in "normal mode" and suddenly life is interrupted by a pause button, crisis, or major transition, our natural reaction is to ask, "Now what?"

Whether it's a global pandemic, a career change, a divorce, the death of a loved one, relocation, retirement, college graduation, a break up, a new ministry, the death of a dream, or the awakening of a new vision—we all come to the place where we ask, "What now? How do I move into my next season?"

Life is a series of transitions from one season to the next. The exit of one season marks the entrance to a new season. Some of these transitions are much more dramatic than others. My wife, Dee, and I are about to move into a seismic transition because in about two weeks, we expect to be first-time grandparents! Dee has already begun to prepare by getting baby equipment for our house and picking what "grandma" name she wants to be called by.

OFTEN WE ARE MORE COMFORTABLE WITH AN OLD PROBLEM THAN WITH A NEW SOLUTION.

What Now? is written to help you step into your next season with confidence and boldness. In the space between seasons, there are moments of chaos, confusion, and uncertainty that lead to change. The transition gap between who you once were and who you are becoming can be intense and unnerving. It is in the transition gap that the biggest mistakes are made and the greatest advancements are achieved. Before and after the gap, there will be seasons that pile up questions and other seasons that dispense clarity and answers.

Many of us become paralyzed by fear or the indecision of moving forward, so we stay in the waiting room of procrastination way too long. Often we are more comfortable with an old problem than with a new solution.

If you are at the edge of a new season reluctantly looking toward the future but not sure how to move forward, then I'm glad you are reading this book.

What Now? will provide you with five key steps to moving forward that every person in transition should consider in order to successfully move into a new season.

My hope is that you would move into your next season at the right time, in the right frame of mind, with a clear vision to transition onward.

Here is a summary of the five steps to moving forward.

1) QUIET YOUR SOUL TO LISTEN

The very first step as you consider moving into a new season is to stop and listen. This seems simple enough, but it is often the most difficult step to take in a world filled with noise and distractions. There is an art to quieting our soul and listening to the still small voice. Who has God uniquely created you to be? What is the essence of your calling? How has God been preparing you for this new season? What is God whispering to you that you must quiet yourself to hear?

2) RE-ENVISION YOUR LIFE STORY

The second step is to revisit your life's story. When you are immersed in one intense chapter of your story, it is hard to see the bigger narrative. Sometimes one painful, disruptive, or traumatic chapter can seem to sabotage your whole story. Moving forward requires erasing a distorted storyboard, sorting through the identity lies and accepting your God-given story line.

3) ADJUST YOUR THINKING

The third step is to adjust your thinking so you can succeed in your new season. The mindset you carry into your new season can either sustain you or derail you. Your mind can convince you of something that isn't really true, and you tell yourself it is an accurate and rational reflection of truth, but it's merely a distortion. Psychologists refer to this as "cognitive distortion." For many, moving to the next season requires a major adjustment to our pattern of thinking.

4) INVITE OTHERS TO YOUR JOURNEY

The fourth step involves inviting others to our journey. The tendency to isolate and insulate ourselves relationally can determine the difference between success and failure in our next season. Embracing community requires a level of vulnerability and transparency that pride and self-sufficiency tend to aggressively resist. You cannot sustain a healthy new season without choosing to embrace the messiness of community.

5) TAKE THE FIRST BOLD STEP

Every journey starts with a first step forward. You will not enter a new season by standing still. When the time is right, every new season is initiated by a bold step forward. A marriage journey is initiated by the bold step of an engagement proposal. A college degree is initiated by the bold step of application and enrollment. A commitment to follow Christ is celebrated by the bold step of public baptism. Often we stop at the border of a new season, reluctant to commit ourselves to the implications of a bold step, but the journey cannot start without it.

What Now? is about how to move into your next season, and much of the content in this book has been adapted from a previous book I wrote titled *Unstuck: Out of Your Cave into Your Call*.

Each chapter breaks down one of the five steps to moving forward. So raise your head, look your future squarely in the eyes, and move forward into your next God-ordained season. Let the journey begin!

CHAPTER 1

YOU CAN'T STAY WHERE YOU ARE

I was only twenty-one, but already I felt stuck. I lay there on my grandmother's floral-patterned couch as waves of discouragement washed over me. Every bone in my body seemed to ache. I had tried as hard as I knew how but was tired of spinning my wheels and going nowhere. I wasn't sure I had the energy or even the desire to continue on. There I was, only five months into my ministry, and I was already physically depleted, emotionally discouraged, and spiritually dry. I had to admit it: I didn't know how to move forward from here.

My mind raced back.

BURNED OUT IN FOUR MONTHS

Only a few months earlier, I had walked slowly up the concrete stairs of the former Russian Orthodox church. It was my first day on the job and there was nobody else in the building. I strolled down the middle aisle to the small makeshift office behind the stage and sat on an old wooden chair. My thoughts were interrupted by the scurrying of squirrel feet on the old tin ceiling. Apparently they liked my preaching and decided to make this their home church.

This small church on the southwest side of Chicago had about eighteen people and could afford to pay me only a minimal part-time salary. They had been looking for a pastor for about two years but were having a difficult time finding anyone willing to accept the salary and live in the neighborhood. In fact, at least one seminary candidate had driven by the building and rolled down his window but refused to get out of his car. Instead, he locked his doors and sped away. Sunday morning we had a piano player to lead the singing, but Sunday night and Wednesdays the group sang a cappella out of hymnbooks. The small leadership committee was so desperate they asked me, a single twenty-one-year-old fresh out of college and with no pastoral experience, to be their pastor. I was naïve enough to say yes. Desperate and naïve—we made a great combination.

A businessman from the congregation felt sorry for me, so he allowed me to stay rent free in a building he owned that was used for offices and warehouse space. I lived in one room and shared the bathroom with the office workers. I had a mattress on the floor and a flimsy table with two yellow vinyl-covered chairs. My books were stacked on the floor and I had mousetraps strategically placed around my mattress to ward off the little rodents that made their rounds at night.

Several families quickly left the mission church after I arrived. Apparently our clapping and my guitar playing during the service were unacceptable to the old guard. So I managed to take a group of twenty down to fifteen in a few short weeks. We had no worship team or functioning Sunday school, and our offerings were pretty pathetic. Our building, constructed in 1910, was falling apart. Gang members hung out on the front steps of the church like they owned the street corner. I was supposed to be getting married in a couple of months and I could barely afford to live on my $8,000-a-year salary myself, let alone support a wife. I had no car of my own, no savings, and no insurance. I had been running hard from early in the morning to late at night with very few visible results to show. *Maybe*, I thought, *I'm not cut out to be a pastor.*

Since I had no insurance, my grandmother's doctor agreed to see me free of charge in the neighboring state of Indiana. I wasn't sure what was wrong, but I knew I was out of energy and feeling drained and my body ached. After examining me, the doctor sternly warned me that I needed bed rest and that my health was at risk if I did not take care of myself. That week on my grandmother's couch, I spent a full day moaning and complaining. I was semi-delirious, battling bouts of fever and drifting in and out of sleep.

"Why have You let this happen, God?" was my faint prayer. "How did I end up here anyway?" Eventually I summoned the strength to wrap myself in a blanket and made my way to the basement. I paced the length of that basement floor and continued grumbling to God that I had done all that He had asked me to and that He had led me to a dead-end situation. I felt stuck and abandoned. The more I complained, the worse I felt. A dark cloud of bleakness settled over my prayers of complaint. In frustration I told God that I did not want to do this anymore. God was silent.

OUT OF THE BASEMENT

The next day I was too exhausted to keep complaining and too worn out to keep moaning. I just lay there wrapped in my blanket, silent before God. Finally, in the silence of that dark basement, the still small whisper of God's voice began to pierce through the confusing noise of my dark spiritual dissonance. I slowly began to realize I had become too busy with my mission to make time to listen to God. The voice of people's needs and my drive to succeed had made me slip away from the most important call—my own walk with God.

Over the next couple of days, I did some deep soul-searching. I began to see some of the unhealthy pressures that were driving me. In addition, I came face-to-face with an ugly arrogance in my soul. I had fallen into the trap of thinking that it was my job to fix people, save people, and meet people's needs.

I caught myself praying, "Forgive me for attempting

to do in my own strength what only You can do in the power of Your Spirit." I gradually came to realize that God didn't need a miniature pseudo-messiah frantically trying to do the work of the real Messiah. I admitted my self-reliance and lack of dependence on God. I felt broken over the arrogance that had led me to such a dark

I FELT BROKEN OVER THE ARROGANCE THAT HAD LED ME TO SUCH A DARK PLACE BUT HUMBLED BY THE AMAZING GRACE OF A GOD WHO WAS DRAWING ME OUT.

place but humbled by the amazing grace of a God who was drawing me out. This was a turning point, a defining moment. When I finally walked up those basement stairs, I knew I had heard the whisper of God's Spirit. A transition was taking place. A new season was starting to emerge.

I decided I could not do ministry the same way anymore. As I drove back to Chicago, I knew change was coming. I was driving back to the same pressure, people problems, and financial crises, but I felt different. I had a new awareness of my own weakness, a consciousness of my dependence on God. In the months that followed, the little church began to experience unexpected breakthroughs.

Suddenly people who had been resistant were now responding. It appeared as though an invisible lid was taken off our struggling congregation. Our worship services were brimming with a new sense of God's presence. What I had failed to do in my frantic self-effort was beginning to happen as I stepped aside and made room for God. People from many backgrounds and diverse neighborhoods in Chicago began making their way to the old brick building on 44th and Paulina. This was the beginning of a new season.

SHAPED BY THE STRUGGLE

That brief but defining "basement" experience helped shape me in profound ways. My personal meltdown impressed upon me the importance of not going ahead of God, nor lagging behind Him, but seeking to stay closely in step with His leading. I have often remembered the painful experience of being too busy for God and the frustration of trying to pursue a mission in my own strength. The early lessons I learned in the struggle to exit that basement and step back into my calling have profoundly shaped my approach to life.

Maybe you have been in your own "basement"—that place you don't want to be in anymore but where God has put you temporarily to prepare you for your next season of life. The "basement" is usually a challenging place, a painful place of self-discovery, and a place where we come face-to-face with our own deficiencies and our need for God's grace.

I think of Joseph, an immature seventeen-year-old who received a God-given dream, but he was not strong enough to carry the weight of that dream. So God allowed him to be thrown into an unexpected crisis through some toxic family drama. He is betrayed and sold into slavery by his very own brothers. A powerful man by the name of Potiphar buys Joseph and puts him to work at his estate. In this "basement" crisis, Joseph is forced to learn hard work, administration skills, delegation, and eventually management abilities. Just about the time that his life seems to be improving, he is falsely accused and thrown into the second phase of crisis called "prison." So he goes from crisis to crisis without taking a break. In prison he learns compassion for other inmates and discovers that he has a God-given ability to interpret dreams. At a "soul level," Joseph has been stripped of his young arrogance and, through pain and perseverance, is being shaped into a leader God can use.

Now he is about thirty years old and finally prepared to carry the weight of his dream and fulfill his calling. In the first part of his crisis, he learned management and leadership abilities. In the second half of his crisis, he discovered gifting he never knew he had. His "basement" experience equipped him with leadership abilities and gift discovery that prepared him for his ultimate calling. Joseph saved his family and rescued a nation from a devastating famine. When Joseph finally reveals his true identity to the brothers who had betrayed him and sold him into slavery, he makes a profound statement: "You intended to harm me, but God intended it for good to accomplish what is now being done, the saving of many lives" (Gen. 50:20).

As I write, our country is going through one of the worst pandemics since the Spanish flu of 1918. Millions of people have been forced to quarantine, stay home from work, and practice social distancing. Schools have shut down, businesses have had to hang "closed" signs on their doors, churches have stopped gatherings, weddings have been postponed, graduations cancelled, and life as we know it has been put on pause. As we move toward "reopening," many are asking, "What will the future look like for me?" Maybe your future will depend on what you learn in the crisis while life is on pause. What dreams are being shaped? What skills are being developed? What character is being strengthened? What is God doing in your life now to prepare you for what may be the most influential season of your life?

As you look back over your own story and try to explain how you ended up where you are, you may discover the same thing I did. There are many events that have affected your journey. Typically it was not one event that got you where you are; it was a series of events—and your response to those events—that led you to your current predicament.

I have seen many vibrant, gifted people unexpectedly end up stalled on the side of the road. They are scratching their heads and wondering what in the world happened to them. Often they linger so long in that spiritual traffic jam that their soul drains, their dreams evaporate, and they dismiss their vision as a season of naïve, youthful idealism.

Millions of Americans are undergoing a period of great testing and deep disruption. There are many questions and uncertainties about the future. Some will flounder and cling to the past in a desperate effort to avoid a new reality. Many will focus on just getting back to "normal." Others will be shaped by the crisis and equipped like never before to embrace a new future.

THE DEFINING MOMENT

Most of us reach a point when we have to decide whether we will continue to cling to the security of an old season or step into the uncertainty of a new one. This is a defining moment. It involves a step of obedience, an act of faith, and trusting our heavenly Father. You will know clearly if you have taken this step or not. I have met many people who know what they should do but live their life in perpetual postponement. They deceive themselves into thinking that they are on the way but actually are stuck waiting for the right timing, resources, or change in circumstances. They live with the illusion of progress but the reality of perpetual postponement.

In the next few chapters, we will take a look at the

five-step process to moving forward. Being willing to work through the progression of transition is what separates those who remain trapped and those who move to their next season.

I don't know your story, but I do know that a new season is within your grasp. I hope you are beginning to hear the spiritual whisper calling you toward the next phase in God's plan for you. That divine undertone, stirring a holy discontent that makes you long to live differently. I pray you find your heart even now being awakened to the possibilities of stepping bravely into your next season.

The first step is to quiet your soul and start to listen to the still small voice.

CHAPTER 2

QUIET YOUR SOUL TO LISTEN

Celebrated film producer Jeffrey Katzenberg asked, "What does God sound like?" I was in Hollywood at the production headquarters of DreamWorks. Twenty other evangelical pastors and I had been invited to preview the film *The Prince of Egypt* and offer our feedback. I felt a little out of place as the youngest pastor there, and in the company of nationally known church leaders. They invited me as a representative of the "younger generation."

From his seat in the DreamWorks conference room,

Katzenberg described the team's most difficult task in creating the epic film. "We had a hard time knowing how to record the voice of God in the burning bush scene," he explained. "We considered the thunder voice approach and the deep baritone 'James Earl Jones' style, but in the end none of those seem to fit." He paused. "Then we had an idea. We took the voices of a hundred different people—men, women, and children—and recorded them into one single voice track."

God's lines were spoken by all the film's lead actors together. Sound engineer Lon Bender directed the actors to whisper the lines, so that none would dominate the performance. He and his team then took the voice of Val Kilmer, who voice-acted Moses, and made his voice louder than the others. As a result, Kilmer gave voice to both Moses and God, suggesting that often we hear God speak to us in our own voice.

The concept of more than a hundred different voices making up the voice of God actually has a prophetic ring to it. God speaks in hundreds of languages to the hearts of people around the world through His Word.

DO YOU HEAR HIM WHEN HE SPEAKS?

Of course we can never know, this side of heaven, what God's voice sounds like exactly. But Scripture tells us clearly that God does speak to us. He has spoken through the prophets and through His Word, and most perfectly through His Son, Jesus Christ (Heb. 1:1–2). The question, then, is not whether God speaks but whether we hear Him when He speaks. If we ever hope to successfully transition from one season to the next, we must learn to quiet our soul, listen attentively, and discern the voice of God when He speaks to us.

In the middle of the COVID-19 pandemic, I began reading Psalm 46 every morning as I watched the sunrise with a strong cup of coffee in my hand. The psalm starts with a reassuring declaration: "God is our refuge and strength, an ever-present help in trouble. Therefore we will not fear." In the middle of a time of elevated death tolls, sickness, economic trouble, and national crisis, my soul needed to meditate on those words each day. What struck me as I read the psalm each morning was that verses 1 and 2 were connected to the practice given to us in verse 10: "Be still, and know that I am God; I will be exalted among the nations, I will be exalted in the earth." Being fearless and grasping that God is our refuge and strength is tied to the practice of being still and knowing. *Be still* means that I have to stop doing, scrolling, planning, talking, watching, and hash-tagging. It means that I stop. I cease activity. It is in the stopping and the stillness that my soul can finally breathe and my spirit can begin to grasp that God is my refuge and strength.

BEING FEARLESS AND GRASPING THAT GOD IS OUR REFUGE AND STRENGTH IS TIED TO THE PRACTICE OF BEING STILL AND KNOWING.

It is in stillness that fear and anxiety start to shrink in the presence of the Great I Am. Stillness allows me to process my thoughts and direct my thinking toward a focus on His Word. It allows me to pause and strengthen my knowing.

Stillness repositions us to hear God's voice more clearly. Just the other day I was on my cellphone talking with my wife, Dee, when her voice became choppy. I had to walk outside the building to find better reception. If I had stayed deep inside the building, my wife's voice would have continued to be unclear. I had to reposition myself before I could hear her clearly again.

When we refuse to respond to His voice, God sometimes uses other means to move us along. Jonah refused to go to Nineveh, so God sent a storm and a man-swallowing fish. The population of earth refused to listen in Noah's day, so God sent the flood. Pharaoh refused to listen, so God sent the plagues.

Often it is the extraordinary interruptions and dramatic wake-up calls that motivate us to reposition ourselves to listen attentively. I have heard many stories of people who, just before they awakened to the voice of God, were startled by a dramatic disruption in their life. A nearly fatal car accident. A difficult and painful divorce. A cancer diagnosis. The collapse of a business venture. The loud, attention-getting sirens are not an end in themselves but merely a warning of what is coming. The flashing lights and siren of the police cars and security vehicles make way for the president's entourage, but the first family is not in the police car. Do not confuse the announcement with the presence.

When I was a young dad, I determined that we would try to eat dinner as a family every evening. Through the teen years it was not always easy to rally the family and get everyone to the table on time. Now I understand why in the old cowboy movies the cook would ring a bell to announce the chow was ready. When my son Grant was a teenager, there were many evenings I would call upstairs to announce that it was dinnertime only to be met with silence. I once walked by the stairs and called out, "Grant, dinner is ready." I waited and heard no answer. In a louder voice I said, "Grant, did you hear me? Dinner is ready." Still no answer.

Increasing my volume significantly, I shouted, "Grant! Can you hear me? Dinner is ready!" Still no answer. Then I banged on the wall closest to his room and said loudly, "Can you hear me?"

This time, from inside his upstairs room, I heard Grant ask, "Dad, did you say something?"

A little irritated, I said, "Yes, this is my fourth time calling you. Why aren't you responding?"

"Oh, I had headphones on. I couldn't hear you."

There you have it. The noise in his ears was louder than my voice, so although I was calling to him with good news (dinnertime), he still couldn't hear me. When the voices in our head are louder than the voice of God, we have a problem. Only the practice of being still will help us turn down the volume in our head to hear the voice of the Holy Spirit.

In the New Testament, Paul reminds us about the challenge of keeping the noise out of our heads. He calls us "to be made new in the attitude of your minds; and to put on the new self, created to be like God in true righteousness and holiness" (Eph. 4:23–24). As we do this, it's important that we "do not give the devil a foothold" (v. 27).

Fear and anger are two of the primary footholds the enemy uses to get noise inside our heads. Anger and fear are irrational emotional cousins that override our logical thinking and, if given the chance, will sabotage our faith as well.

Psychologist and author Henry Cloud describes this tendency in his book *Boundaries for Leaders*. He emphasizes the fact that leaders need to set boundaries on their tendency to allow single events or results to define them. Sometimes one difficult event can set a domino reaction in motion. We take an event personally, we think it is pervasive, and we believe it will be permanent. Cloud describes the conversation we have when fear starts to get a grip in these terms. "Personalizing: 'I am not good enough to pull this off. It's going to be terrible. They won't like me.' Pervasive: 'Everything is going south. Nothing we are doing is working and this will not either.' Permanent: 'It's not going to be any different tomorrow. It will always be the same as it is now.'"[1]

Perhaps you have allowed a trigger event in your life to overwhelm you. Maybe you have allowed an event or incident to open a door that you cannot close. It has become the negative door prop in your life. You don't get the job promotion, and fear props the door open. Your boyfriend says it's not going to work out, and the anxiety noise gets louder. Your son comes back with a bad report card, and the worry volume rises. Whatever message gets a foothold inside your head and is repeated at a high volume will shape your future thinking. The real challenge becomes when the noise inside your head is so loud that it drowns out the sound of God.

THE SOUND OF GOD

Three chapters into the Bible we find the first record of people responding to the attention-grabbing sound of

God before they actually hear His voice. God was looking for Adam and Eve in the garden.

> "Then the man and his wife heard the sound of the LORD God as he was walking in the garden in the cool of the day, and they hid from the LORD God among the trees of the garden." (Gen. 3:8)

Notice this verse says they "heard the *sound* of the LORD God as he was walking in the garden." Not the voice of God, but the sound of God. I am not sure what God sounds like when He walks. I do know, however, that God can be as loud or as quiet as He wants to be. Clearly God chose to make Himself heard as He walked through the garden that day. He knew that Adam and Eve were hiding and gave them an opportunity to respond to His arrival. He virtually stomps His feet through the garden, announcing His presence before He speaks. "But the LORD God called to the man, 'Where are you?' He answered, 'I heard you in the garden, and I was afraid because I was naked; so I hid'" (Gen. 3:9–10).

Instead of emerging from their hiding place with arms open wide and admitting their failure, the first couple hid from God's presence, driven by guilt, fear, and shame.

In a similar way, God announces His presence at key times in our life. Not just when it's time to discipline, but when He wants us to hear Him clearly. He stomps His feet, clears His throat, and lets us know God is in the house. His deliberate *sound* is a preparation for His *voice*.

THE PRACTICE OF STILLNESS

Several years ago we partnered with an overcrowded public school in our neighborhood to create classroom space for 165 kindergarten children. I was impressed with how well-behaved these children were. One day I walked past twenty-five naturally rowdy Chicago kindergarten boys and girls. They were walking in pairs with the teacher at the front of the line. You could have heard a pin drop as they walked the hallway. This veteran teacher had developed a technique to make normally chaotic hallways orderly and quiet. All the children walked with their hands clasped together and their two index fingers over their lips, which reminded them that this was a no-talking and no-touching zone. The only voice I heard was the voice of the teacher quietly giving them instructions.

That is a compelling picture of the practice of stillness. Chaos, confusion, and stress can become our normal unless we learn how to silence the voices, put our fingers over our lips, and hear only the holy whisper as we walk the hallways of life quietly toward His presence.

For years I have been practicing a morning ritual of being still and knowing. Not everyone is wired the same, so this might not be the best format for you, but for me it is spiritually life-giving. There are four key components to my "be still and know" morning rhythm.

1) A Quiet Space to Listen

I'm a morning person and usually the first person awake in my household. My quiet space has varied over the years, but I prefer a place that is quiet and facing the sunrise so I can see and feel the sun as it rises.

2) The Word to Reflect

God speaks clearly and most powerfully through His revealed Word known as Scripture. In the morning I read Scripture asking two questions: "Lord, what are You saying to me?" and "Is there anything You want me to do about it?"

3) Journal to Process

Since the age of seventeen, I have engaged in the habit of journaling. It helps me process the lessons I'm learning and not forget what He has taught me.

4) Prayer to Connect

Through prayer I connect with my heavenly Father. It's personal, heartfelt, real, and open. Prayer is the most intimate and intense part of "being still and knowing."

Let me reiterate that being still and meditating on the hum of a hummingbird or the sound of the wind is not the intent of the psalmist. That may have some relaxation benefit, but it does not renew us spiritually. The focal point of being still is to know that He is God and to listen without interruption to His voice.

I know that some of you may be thinking that your life is way too busy for a morning ritual like I just described. Maybe you're a mother with small children and you barely have time to brush your teeth without being interrupted.

As a college student, I read a short booklet that had a deep impact on my life. Brother Lawrence, author of

The Practice of the Presence of God, was a Carmelite monk who worked in a busy kitchen at the monastery where he served. Lawrence wrote,

> There is not in the world a kind of life more sweet and delightful, than that of a continual conversation with God; those only can comprehend it who practice and experience it; yet I do not advise you to do it from that motive; it is not pleasure which we ought to seek in this exercise; but let us do it from a principle of love, and because God would have us.[2]

What Brother Lawrence learned is that he could live in constant awareness of the presence of God even in the midst of a noisy, busy kitchen.

We cannot tell God how and when to speak to us. We can, however, position ourselves to hear His voice. As long as we stay locked in our basement, blasting the noise of fear and anger, we will not hear His voice. Maybe it is time for you to embrace your own ritual of being still and knowing that He is God. So turn down the white noise and turn up the God volume.

CHAPTER 3

RE-ENVISION YOUR LIFE STORY

One day I received a phone call from a representative of a local university. I had been recommended to offer the invocation at their graduation ceremony. I felt honored that I was being asked to participate in this internationally attended ceremony at the prestigious Rockefeller Chapel on the campus of the University of Chicago.

The call came about two years into my ministry. I was starting to struggle with my life "storyboard." In the film industry, a storyboard is a sequence of drawings that lays out the narrative flow of a movie. Before the movie is ever produced, the storyboard gives the director a visual picture of where it is going. I was wrestling to make sense of my own storyboard at the time. While my college friends were leaving Chicago to travel to exciting ministries in exotic places, I was staying put. The church was growing and people were being changed, but we were still small and struggling. I was starting my ministry in a neighborhood that most people were trying to leave. The people we were reaching in those days were mainly addicts, felons, and the marginalized. I was wrestling to make ends meet financially and my young wife had to work a full-time job just to keep us afloat. I shopped at thrift stores, fixed my car on the street, found furniture in alleyways, had no insurance, and had ongoing altercations with neighborhood gangbangers. For the first three months of my marriage, my wife and I slept on the floor because we could not afford a bed. I never heard her complain—not once—but the pressure of finances and stress of city ministry was tough.

When I arrived at the Rockefeller Chapel, I looked up at the magnificent structure, the tallest building on the University of Chicago campus. The façade was decorated with more than one hundred stone sculptures, representing philosophy and the humanities, religion and university life. I was greeted cordially by the event coordinator, who quickly told me what an important event this was. He reminded me that people had traveled from around the world to attend this ceremony. They had an impressive list of distinguished guests participating in the event. We went into the green room, where I met the college president and other faculty. I put on a long black robe and we briskly made our way up the side aisle to the platform. On our way, the coordinator reminded me that this was a nonsectarian event and there would be people from many religious backgrounds at this gathering. He said I had the reputation of being an intelligent young pastor, so he knew I would understand if he asked me not to be sectarian in my comments. When I asked what exactly he meant, he said I should keep my prayers generic so as not to offend anyone in attendance. Reference to Jesus Christ would make people feel uncomfortable, so words like "God" or "Supreme Being" would be more appropriate in this setting. Before I could respond, we were ushered onto the stage.

I sat on the platform facing the international crowd. I could see that there were many ethnicities represented. I glanced at the stately elegance of this historic chapel and thought, *What a contrast to the little church I preach in on Sundays!* This chapel was filled with the elite of society. I spent my days working with felons and addicts.

I snapped out of my thoughts when I heard the master of ceremonies announce, "And now we have Reverend Jobe, who will lead us in an invocation to start today's ceremony."

I stepped to the podium, cleared my throat, looked out at the crowd, and prayed a generic, bland, nonsectarian prayer. The event coordinator nodded approvingly as I walked back to my seat. As soon as I sat down, I felt a wave of conviction flood my spirit. What flashed through my mind were Paul's words: "For I am not ashamed of the gospel, because it is the power of God that brings salvation to everyone who believes: first to the Jew, then to the Gentile" (Rom. 1:16).

I had started living with a storyboard in which I saw myself as a poor, forgotten inner-city pastor who would spend his years struggling in obscurity. That storyboard drove me to seek acceptance at the expense of my core values.

That day on the prestigious Rockefeller Chapel platform, I repented before God. I was oblivious to what any speaker said behind the podium that morning. I was preoccupied with an intense internal conversation. Then I heard a voice say, "And now, Reverend Jobe will bring our time to an end with a closing benediction."

I practically jumped to my feet. As I approached the podium I saw a different picture. Instead of a poor, forgotten little pastor stuck in life, I saw a picture of a bold servant of God not bending to the pressure of denying the name of Jesus. I stood up with new courage and fresh confidence. I said, "I know this is a nonsectarian event. My intention is not to offend anyone. But I will pray in the only name I know how to pray, the name of Jesus." This time I prayed with authority and assurance in the name of Jesus Christ. When I finished praying, I did not wait to get a nod from the event coordinator. I quickly made my way down the aisle with my robes swishing behind me.

I DETERMINED BEFORE GOD THAT DAY THAT I WOULD NEVER ALLOW THE PRESSURE OF SOCIETY TO SILENCE THE POWER OF HIS NAME FROM MY LIPS.

Halfway down the aisle a young woman stepped out in front of me. "Reverend Jobe," she said.

"Yes?" I braced myself for a verbal assault.

"Thank you," she said. "I have been at several graduation ceremonies and never once has the pastor had the courage to pray in Jesus' name. Thank you for your courage."

That day I learned an important lesson. I realized how easily my warped mental storyboard affects how I see myself and how I behave under pressure. I determined before God that day that I would never allow the pressure of society to silence the power of His name from my lips.

Our perception of reality affects the way we live and act. Often the mental picture we carry to define our reality does not match God's picture. Only when we discover the storyboard that is defining our life and align it with God's storyboard can we begin to live on target with the mission of God.

REFRESH YOUR STORYBOARD

Abraham is a prime example of the power of living by a divine picture. Abraham and Sarah, his wife, were childless. God promised Abraham that one day he would be the father of a great nation. As the years passed, Abraham struggled to maintain his faith and cling to the promise God had given him. Since Abraham remained childless, he offered to fulfill this promise through his servant Eliezer of Damascus. God responded to Abraham emphatically, "This man will not be your heir; but one who will come forth from your own body, he shall be your heir" (Gen. 15:4 NASB).

To strengthen Abraham's faith, God gave him a new mental picture. He took Abraham out on a clear Middle Eastern night and invited Abraham to look to the stars, and said, "Now look toward the heavens, and count the stars, if you are able to count them." God added, "So shall your descendants be" (Gen. 15:5 NASB).

To strengthen Abraham's faith, God had to give him a fresh mental picture, a new storyboard. From that moment on, Abraham revisited the picture of a sky filled with stars to strengthen his faith. I can imagine that in moments of discouragement, Abraham closed his eyes and remembered the sight of thousands of stars, and the voice of God saying, "So shall your descendants be."

This new, clear image was Abraham's defining storyboard. Much of what the Scriptures seek to do is to erase misleading images built on faulty distortions and repaint new images based on God's truth and perspective.

THE KNOWLEDGE OF THE HOLY

My first semester at college was difficult. I wrestled with what I wanted to do with my life and future. I had a part-time job working for a doctor who owned a boating magazine and lived in an exclusive neighborhood in downtown Chicago. After numerous conversations with my boss, I began to doubt whether I should come back to Bible college the next semester. I had no idea what I would do after my schooling, and I began to feel like I should have a "real degree" to survive in the "real world." The doctor, who was not a Christian, questioned why I was wasting a sharp mind just studying the Bible and theology. He reasoned, "You can have your faith, but you need a career to make a living." When the semester ended, I was hired for a summer job at a hotel in a coastal town in southern France.

Someone had given me a copy of A. W. Tozer's *The Knowledge of the Holy*. After work I would jog down to the oceanfront, take a swim, and read from the book. It wasn't the ideal place to read *The Knowledge of the Holy* since beaches in southern France are not known for their modesty. But that summer I realized that the pathway to understanding my purpose started with understanding my Creator. Tozer put it this way:

> What comes into our minds when we think about God is the most important thing about us.
>
> The history of mankind will probably show that no people has ever risen above its religion, and man's spiritual history will positively demonstrate that no religion has ever been greater than its idea of God. Worship is pure or base as the worshiper entertains high or low thoughts of God.[1]

I needed to see my storyboard clearly in the light of a fresh understanding of the magnitude of God. My thought pattern that had become distorted by my own insecurities and influenced by a well-meaning but materialistic doctor needed to be exposed to the knowledge of God. That summer was a turning point. I had to answer the question: "What are you doing here, Mark?" For most of the summer, I wrestled to answer that question. Before the summer was over, I knelt as an eighteen-year-old and surrendered my future to the lordship of Jesus. I remember the freedom I felt surrendering control of my own storyboard and being willing to embrace God's plan.

The longer you live with the wrong storyboard, the harder it is to erase. That is why many men or women who've had dysfunctional childhoods have such a hard time erasing distorted images of themselves and their world. They have lived with a lie-based image so long that it warps their identity and worldview. I have had countless conversations with women who struggle with understanding the love of their heavenly Father because of their dysfunctional relationship with their abusive earthly father.

Scripture tells us that the key to transformation is the renewing of our mind. "Do not conform to the pattern of this world, but be transformed by the renewing of your mind. Then you will be able to test and approve what God's will is—his good, pleasing and perfect will" (Rom. 12:2). Our storyboard will always be misrepresented until we properly see God in the bigger picture of our board.

What storyboard are you currently living with? Is it a mental picture that contradicts the picture that God has declared over you? Take a moment to visually erase the image that is defining your life. Now allow God to redraw a new mental picture. Let the Master Artist craft His image for you and your life. Can you see it begin to emerge? It is carefully and painstakingly painted with you in mind. The sovereign God of the universe is embedding in your spirit His divine portrait. You have a purpose and a God-given destiny. Prepare to live in this new storyboard.

CHAPTER 4

ADJUST YOUR THINKING

I was a pastor in my twenties in over my head. I knew I needed help, so I called Jake (not his real name) and asked him to move to Chicago and join me. I knew that he had a calling on his life and a sincere passion for God. Jake was very gifted and eager to serve, but he struggled with the voices from his past. He grew up in a broken household with parents who fought through multiple divorces. The scars of dysfunction manifested in Jake as a hypersensitive conscience and a sense of inadequacy that bombarded him with guilt and accusations any time he stepped into new opportunities.

Jake started out with enthusiasm in his new ministry

role. But soon he began to experience unhealthy guilt and chronic feelings of condemnation. Jake and I had long talks about his struggle but nothing seemed to be helping. After several months the pressure was more than he could bear. Unannounced, he packed up his little grey Ford Escort and tried to escape Chicago. On his way out of the city he was struck with a sudden pain in his side that forced him to pull the car to the side of the road. Sensing God was trying to get his attention, but determined to run anyway, he made his way onto the expressway and drove about forty-five minutes outside of Chicago when his car abruptly broke down. He managed to turn the car around and barely made it back to the city. The mechanic that looked at his engine commented, "It must have been God that kept this car running, because this engine is shot." Jake returned to Chicago discouraged and disappointed.

Often what drives us to the paralyzing place of isolation, frustration, and fear are the voices in our head that speak to us about our identity and destiny. The message becomes a script that we repeat to ourselves like a bad recording, over and over, until it becomes our new reality. This is what happened to Jake. Maybe that's what happened to you.

HOW DID YOU GET HERE?

Every person struggling to move forward must answer this question: "What am I doing here?" To answer this question, you will have to rewind and remember what drove you to this place in the first place. As you rewind your story, you will naturally focus on the difficult circumstances and challenging people, but the real focus should be on your thinking. What drives us to the basement is not the people or circumstances but rather our faulty thinking. It's not what happens to us but how our thinking is affected by what happens to us.

In the Old Testament book of Judges, we are introduced to a young man with a strong calling on his life but also heavy baggage. His name is Gideon. For seven years he has lived in an oppressive culture of fear and abuse under a people called the Midianites. Judges 6:5b–6 says "they invaded the land to ravage it. Midian so impoverished the Israelites that they cried out to the LORD for help."

I have worked in the inner city of Chicago for several decades and I have seen the hollow stares of young men imprisoned in cycles of poverty, abuse, and hopelessness. The brutal effect of dysfunctional family life, poverty, and a culture of violence has deeply shaped the identity of many potential leaders. Their broken world speaks so loudly and pervasively that their identity is warped by the overwhelming volume.

Although not the inner city of Chicago, Gideon had grown up in a similar oppressive environment. But everything changes when Gideon has an unexpected encounter with God, and the first tension that comes to light is his own identity. God addresses him as a "mighty warrior." Gideon responds by pointing out that his clan is the weakest and that he is the least in his family. Notice that God sees a mighty warrior and Gideon, when he looks in the mirror, simply sees a weak, vulnerable, and small nobody.

WHAT HAD BEEN A PART OF HIS SHAMEFUL PAST BECOMES THE FUEL TO LIGHT THE ALTAR OF GOD.

As God prepares Gideon to embrace his new identity and shed his inferiority complex, He calls him to do something that is filled with powerful symbolic significance.

Gideon's father, Joash, was the caretaker of the pagan altar of Baal and the Asherah pole. Gideon had grown up with this being part of his family story and heritage. God asked him to take a bold step and tear down the altar of Baal and cut down the Asherah pole. He then instructs

Gideon to build a new altar using the wood from the Asherah pole to light the fire to the altar of God. That became a defining moment. We can almost see the identity shift taking place. In fact, Joash gave him a new name. Gideon, which means "Barley Eater," just didn't seem appropriate any more. Gideon's name is changed to Jerubbaal, which means, "Let Baal contend against him" or "one who fights with Baal."

Notice that what had been a part of his shameful past becomes the fuel to light the altar of God. The very wood that blasphemed the name of God in his family was now the fuel that honored God in the present. I have seen this story repeated hundreds of times. *Sometimes the greatest heat of passion comes from the deepest place of hurt and shame.* God uses the wood of our shameful past to fuel a fire and passion for His honor. The addict that struggled for years with drug abuse now helps others break the chains of addiction.

THE VICTIM MINDSET

One of the most common forms of distorted thinking is a victim mentality. You will inevitably stay stuck when you start believing that you are a victim and that you are not responsible for where you find yourself or for moving forward to what's next.

It is true that we cannot always control what people do against us. We have little power over other people's attitude or behavior toward us. But we can always choose whether or not we take on a victim mentality.

As a father, you are not responsible for the rebellious attitude of your teenage son, but you are responsible for your harshness and anger toward him. As a wife, you are not responsible for the insensitivity and thoughtlessness of your husband, but you are responsible for the bitterness and resentment you allow to grow in your heart as a result. As an employee, you are not responsible for the bad choices your boss makes in the workplace, but you are responsible for the critical outlook you allow to rob your energy and productivity. As a daughter-in-law, you are not responsible for the controlling insecurity of your mother-in-law, but you are responsible for how you allow anger to influence your reactions. As a college student, you are not responsible for the nasty divorce your parents are going through, but you are responsible for the lack of forgiveness you allow to invade your life. As a boss, you are not responsible for the negative attitude of certain employees, but you are responsible for your dismissive or harsh reactions toward them.

It is one thing to fall into occasional distorted thinking, but it takes a personal toll when we get stuck there.

THE TRIGGER POINT

The term "trigger point" was coined in 1942 by physician and medical researcher Dr. Janet Travell to describe a painful point in the human body that, when touched, triggers a twitch response or pain in another part of the body.

The thinking that can keep us from moving forward is gradual and progressive, but it usually has a "trigger point" that, when touched, causes a reaction in another part of our life.

You may be doing great for years when suddenly your trigger point is touched. Your wife mentions divorce, you find pot in your teenage son's backpack, your employer hands out pink slips, you are diagnosed with cancer, a trusted leader disappoints you. A trigger point can unleash a flood of negative emotions that inundates your thinking and drowns your hope. If you have never experienced a serious trigger event, it may seem irrational, but fear is never rational.

Whatever message is repeated the most and the loudest in your head will determine your reflex response to life. The more time we spend alone with our negative or distorted thoughts, the more real and entrenched they become in our thinking.

But there is hope.

RESTART YOUR THINKING

Although Jake attempted to run from Chicago, he ended up right back where he began and was forced to reexamine his own journey.

Jake determined it was time to stop running. It was time to work on hearing the voice of God over the voice of guilt. He committed to do everything possible to reboot his thinking.

Jake began the painful process of reviewing the journey that led him to his place of desperation. He revisited the deep-rooted hurts and issues he had been running from. One day while walking and praying in a local park, he opened up his fist and released the people who had hurt him deeply. With his palm stretched open before God, he committed to not hold on to the hurt anymore. He began to carry with him Scripture written on note cards, passages that spoke of the promises of God and Jake's own identity in Christ. Every time he heard the voice of guilt and condemnation, he quickly pulled out a card and started reading until the negative voice was drowned out. For months he carried these cards in his pocket, posted them on his mirror, kept them on the dashboard of his car. In the beginning he had to review them dozens of times each day. Progress was very slow. But with time he discovered he was starting to build an automatic response to the distorted thinking. Each time it surfaced, the grace-filled truth he was meditating on kicked in. Jake will be the first to admit that this process took time and the battle was intense, but in time his thinking was rebooted. Jake has now walked for years as a faith-filled leader without shying away from challenges and opportunities. Turning up the volume of God's voice and turning down the volume of his misguided script was the beginning of adjusting his thinking.

CHAPTER 5

INVITE OTHERS TO YOUR JOURNEY

Your journey toward the next phase in God's calling for your life begins by confronting the thinking that threatens to hold you back. Now is the time to wrestle with the question God is whispering to you: "What are you doing here?"

In cities like Chicago, you can be surrounded by people, competing for parking spaces, crowding into elevators, bumping into strangers on sidewalks, and living with very little space between you and your neighbors, yet still feel strangely alone. You can be a stay-at-home mom with children clinging to your housecoat, a college student with two thousand Twitter followers, a doctor who sees dozens of patients a day, or a bus driver who interacts with hundreds of people every shift, and still feel isolated. In fact, the most painful loneliness is the kind we experience when people surround us. Most people living in crowded Chicago condos rarely know their next-door neighbors. They share walls, hallways, elevators, and a common building address but remain strangely isolated from each other. Loneliness is not due to the absence of people but to the lack of authentic connection with people.

THE URGE TO ISOLATE

Elijah the prophet from Tishbe (pronounced Tish-bee) lived in the ninth century BC during an especially dark and turbulent time in Israel. King Ahab was the most egocentric and spineless king to sit on the throne of Israel (1 Kings 21:25–26). He married a woman named Jezebel, the infamous daughter of the king of Sidon. Ahab and Jezebel's marriage hurled the northern kingdom into a dark season dominated by worship of Jezebel's personal favorite god, Baal.

Elijah made the gutsy move of confronting Ahab and

pronouncing an epic drought on the land that ended up lasting more than three full years. Ahab declared Elijah the number-one enemy of the state and launched a national manhunt for the elusive prophet. After three years in hiding, Elijah challenged 450 pagan prophets on Mount Carmel to a showdown. Everyone turned out for the big event. There on the summit of the mountain, Elijah sternly rebuked the people of Israel for wavering in their allegiance between God and Baal. The people of Israel agreed they would serve the one who proved he was most powerful by sending fire from heaven. God showed up and Elijah won in spectacular fashion. The entire nation saw Elijah and his God vindicated.

It appeared that Elijah had accomplished his purpose, won the battle, and could ultimately put this three-year ordeal behind him. He could finally stop hiding, go back to his home, put on his favorite slippers, and return to life as usual. He couldn't wait to hear Jezebel give her concession speech. Instead, a messenger came out to meet Elijah with a grim message from the queen: she would kill him within twenty-four hours.

It happened suddenly. It was as if something cracked inside his soul. This spiritual superhero began to melt.

Jezebel's threat gripped Elijah to his very core. The exhilaration of yesterday's victory came crashing down around him. Unshakable faith gave way to uncontrollable fear. Stunned and reeling from Jezebel's message, Elijah turned and ran for his life. For upwards of eight hours, he stumbled through the dry, rocky countryside. The farther he traveled, the more isolated the countryside became. He spotted a broom tree—a shrub with a broad canopy of leaves—and plopped down under its branches. Then he hoarsely whispered a desperate prayer through his heavy breathing: "'I have had enough, Lord,' he said. 'Take my life; I am no better than my ancestors'" (1 Kings 19:4).

Look closely at the story of Elijah and you will notice that for three years leading up to his crisis of faith, he appears very isolated. He was on the run from authorities and undoubtedly had to hide his identity from his neighbors, which I'm sure didn't help. He was forced to live in a sparsely populated area away from his family and friends. On top of that, when Jezebel threatened him, he fled and abandoned the only person who had been at his side: his assistant.

Elijah is not the only one who faced a temptation to isolate. In our modern world, people are visiting one another less frequently and having friends over less frequently. In short, every objective measurement of participation in community is declining.

WE HAVE CREATED A CULTURE IN WHICH PEOPLE ARE HYPER CONNECTED BUT ODDLY ALONE.

Trend forecaster and marketing consultant Faith Popcorn (yes, that's her real name) first used the word "cocooning" in the 1990s. Cocooning refers to the trend of people retreating into their homes and socializing less and less face-to-face. When Popcorn predicted this trend, she could not have understood how quickly technology would make cocooning easier than ever before. Our connectivity has increased through Twitter, texting, Facebook, Instagram, Snapchat, and dozens of other social media platforms and apps, but our sense of belonging seems to be at an all-time low. We have created a culture in which people are hyperconnected but oddly alone.

During the COVID-19 crisis, we were required to practice social distancing, directed to work remotely, and out of necessity had to embrace online meetings. Initially many employees celebrated being able to work from home and avoid their lengthy commute, but as time went on, most people have felt the deteriorating effects of isolation. The number of people struggling with anxiety, depression, loneliness, and suicidal thoughts surged. We were created for community. As human beings, our God-given design is to flourish in relational community. Community is our natural habitat. Isolation eventually has devastating effects on the human soul.

In the past few decades, feelings of loneliness have skyrocketed: 40 percent of adults in two recent surveys said they were lonely, up from 20 percent in the 1980s.[1] A study by the American Council of Life Insurance reported that the loneliest group in America are college students. Surrounded by people their own age and busy with an unending slew of activities and interaction, behind closed doors they admit their extreme loneliness. In fact, college students rank as lonelier than divorced people, welfare recipients, single mothers, rural students, housewives, and the elderly.[2]

ISOLATION AND INSULATION

Isolation and insulation are major issues afflicting our culture. They are also major forces that keep us from moving forward.

Isolation has to do with getting away from people, and insulation has to do with protecting and shielding ourselves from people.

There is a difference between the spiritual discipline of solitude and unhealthy isolation. Wayne Cordeiro, author of *Leading on Empty*, says, "Solitude is a healthy and prescriptive discipline; isolation is a symptom of emotional depletion."[3]

Isolation is the consequence of retreating from those whose help we need in times of trouble. It is the first of two critical errors we can make when we face difficult life challenges. The second is insulation. Isolation leads us to get away from people, but insulation drives us to protect and shield ourselves from people. It's the opposite of vulnerability and transparency. It is a strange paradox that at our point of greatest need, most of us tend to hide from our greatest resource—relationships.

One of the challenges of the recent pandemic is that our churches were not allowed to gather in person, so the majority of churches went to online services. Small groups could no longer meet face-to-face, so we transitioned to video conferencing. This was necessary to prevent the spread of the virus, but the side effect was many people felt isolated at a time when they most needed community. I performed a funeral online via Zoom for a dear woman that passed away due to COVID-19 complications. The family was appreciative for my involvement, but I walked away feeling a sense of loss at not being able to hug the family members and be there physically.

IT IS A STRANGE PARADOX THAT AT OUR POINT OF GREATEST NEED, MOST OF US TEND TO HIDE FROM OUR GREATEST RESOURCE—RELATIONSHIPS.

To move forward, we need to understand the importance of healthy relationships in our life and work.

DREADING MONDAYS?

Working with people in tough neighborhoods in cities like Chicago can be brutal. The turnover rate among pastors, counselors, social workers, and law enforcement is high. Burnout is a widespread problem. Many people become so overwhelmed with the immensity of the needs and intensity of the problems that they quit or they harden themselves to the point that they simply go through the motions in their jobs. A small minority discovers the power of healthy relationships. I am convinced that the leaders who survive long-term are those who intentionally build or find enduring community.[4]

Many people dread Monday mornings. I've heard that most pastors who submit resignations do so on Monday morning, often following a difficult and discouraging Sunday. After being involved in intense urban ministry for a few years and seeing this pattern in ministry, I decided I would try to change the "Monday morning syndrome" for our team of pastors. Instead of taking a day off on Mondays like many pastors do, I organized a Monday morning meeting. The focus was to celebrate together, share the wins from the weekend, worship as a team, pray together and refocus on our mission. Those Monday meetings became lifesavers to many on our leadership team. Many discovered the life-giving power of community through these Monday meetings.

The healthy "long-termers" that maintain their sanity, enjoy healthy marriages, and still love their job are those who have discovered the power of a connected community.

In his book *Boundaries for Leaders*, Henry Cloud summarizes the Second Law of Thermodynamics: "Everything in the universe is running down, running out of energy, and becoming less organized." He applies this law to people and their relational health. People will also run down, run out of energy, and become less focused if they have no input. He points out that in a closed system, where there is no relational input, this running out of energy is inevitable, but in an open system this process can be reversed. Dr. Cloud encourages his readers to "set a boundary on your tendency to be a 'closed system,' and open yourself to outside inputs that bring you energy and guidance."[5]

Maybe as you read this chapter you realized that you are living in isolation, but you are wondering what you can do to break out. I encourage you to start with three simple steps.

First, start with what you already have. You may already have friends in your inner circle who would make great confidants. List your three closest friends. Have a conversation with each of them and explore what it would take to get together once a month. Make your meetings informal and transparent and give each other permission to ask the hard questions.

Second, think of a few people that work or volunteer

with you. Do you have some colleagues you can share responsibility with? Do you have coworkers you can partner with to help you grow and learn from each other? These relationships will not be as personal as your relationship with your confidants, but they can be very supportive.

Third, take a step to invest in a community of faith. Find a local church you can join and in which you can use your gifts and talents to help make a difference. Fight the urge to be critical or think that no one else is like you. Roll up your sleeves and find a place to serve and be on mission together.

Not too long ago my wife received a card from one of her friends that is part of our leadership team:

Dee, It's been on my mind to send you a thank-you card for a while. You have been by my side every dark step of the way through my anxiety. Knowing that you were just a phone call away, ready to read Scripture to me and pray for me, was a huge comfort. Thank you for being there for me each and every morning and for speaking truth to me when irrational fears threatened to take over. It means a lot to know that you went through your own season of fear and anxiety and that you've learned how to give those fears to God and train your mind to quickly move on from fear to truth. Thank you for praying me through and never losing hope for my future.

As you prepare to move into a new season, don't neglect the input of mature, seasoned friends who know you well and can speak into your transition. The power of a friend is irreplaceable. We don't realize how much we need community until we go through a dark season. It is in those moments that we realize isolation is not conquered by simply waiting for life to change. Isolation is overcome when we take steps to lower our guard, open our life, and intentionally invite others to our journey.

CHAPTER 6

TAKE THE
FIRST BOLD STEP

The Mexican policeman in dark sunglasses leaned in closer to my car window. He rested his hand on his revolver, and asked a question that shocked me. I did a double take and asked, somewhat confused, "Excuse me, what did you just say?"

I was speaking at a conference in San Diego, and I asked some friends to come along to enjoy the Southern California weather for a weekend. After the conference, my friend John had an idea. He and his wife had never crossed the border into Mexico and were excited to take advantage of the opportunity. We decided to cross the border for the afternoon and have lunch at a seafood place near Tijuana.

We went to the nearest car rental office to lease a car for the day. The attendant advised me to be careful crossing the border. "Once you cross the border, it's a different world," he warned. He related how just the week before a couple had rented a vehicle to do the same thing we were doing. The local police in Tijuana stopped them and ordered them out of the car. The police entered their car and proceeded to drive off, leaving the couple stranded on the side of the road. We thanked the attendant and promised to be careful. Six of us drove in the minivan across the border with no incident. We enjoyed an authentic meal at a quaint Mexican restaurant near the ocean. We finished our meal, strolled around the town, and enjoyed a relaxing afternoon. When it was time to head back, I drove the van back toward the border crossing.

We were in a lively conversation, laughing and joking, when one of the passengers said, "Hey, there's a policeman following you."

I laughed and said, "Yeah, right." I adjusted my mirror and saw a Mexican motorcycle policeman following closely behind me. I put my turn signal on and casually switched lanes. The policeman followed right behind me. Then, to the dismay of everyone in our van, he starting flashing his lights and motioning us to pull over. I reluctantly pulled to the side of the road. The officer dismounted his motorcycle and approached the driver's side window. He wore a helmet and dark sunglasses, and a revolver hung from a holster on his hip.

He looked first at me and then glanced at the other passengers in the vehicle before he ordered me to pull into the side street ahead. As I pulled onto the side road, my passengers warned me to be careful and to be ready to take off if necessary. The officer asked for my documentation matter-of-factly. He said he was going to have to take me down to the police station to pay a fine, because I had been speeding a few miles down the road. I expressed my surprise that he couldn't simply write me a ticket. He shook his head ominously. He continued to ask questions and stall for time, as if he were waiting for me to offer him a bribe. When I told him I was a pastor in Chicago, he paused and looked at me seriously. Then he said something that caught me totally off guard.

This Mexican policeman in dark sunglasses leaned in closer to my window, rested his hand on his revolver, and asked me somberly, "What does Romans 13 say?"

I did a double take. I wasn't sure I had heard him correctly. "Excuse me, sir, what did you just say?"

"What does Romans 13 say?" he repeated.

Two thoughts immediately raced through my mind. First was, *What in the world* does *Romans 13 say?* Second was, *If I don't pass this Bible quiz, I may end up in a Mexican prison.* I fumbled for words, stalling for time to remember Romans 13. "Well," I said, "Romans 12 tells us not to be conformed to this world."

He looked at me and it was obvious he was not impressed. Then I remembered the general gist of Romans 13. I blurted out, "Romans 13 says to submit to the governing authorities since they are servants of God." He immediately took off his sunglasses and shook my hand. For the rest of our conversation, he referred to me as "pastor." He told me to watch the way I drive and be careful in this town. As he walked back to his motorcycle, I sat stunned. He rode his motorcycle up beside my car and said, "Pastor, tell your congregation in Chicago to pray for the police department in Tijuana. We really need it."

Then he rode off.

I buckled my seat belt, looked in the rearview mirror,

and carefully pulled away. It dawned on me that I had crossed the border into a different country and culture, but God was not limited by human borders. He had given me the tools to move across borders and equipped me before I knew it. What are the chances that a guy from Chicago would speak Spanish and know what Romans 13 says?

Some of you reading these pages are standing at the edge of something new and contemplating your first step across the border. I want to remind you that God has already gone before you. Stepping out may stretch your faith, but God is already preparing a way.

The first bold step never comes without challenges. Crossing borders, stepping into new seasons, and walking through open doors will always stretch our faith and challenge our comfort. The moment you step out into a new environment, the adventure begins.

Some people have been crippled so long that it has warped their whole person. The gospel of Luke introduces us to a woman who was stuck for eighteen long years. For almost two decades, she was bent over with severe curvature of her spine so crippling that her daily activities were a constant challenge. No doubt eating, drinking, and even walking were extremely difficult. Constant pain was her everyday companion. Her relationships, her finances, her health, her identity, her spiritual state were all deeply affected by her condition.

While her medical issue was undeniably physical, the root of her problem was spiritual. She had a spiritual problem that affected her soul and her body as well. Luke, the author of this gospel and the book of Acts, was also a doctor, and he uses interesting words to diagnose her condition. He doesn't use the word that would mean "illness, disease, or injury." Instead he uses the phrase "crippled by a spirit."

Scripture says, "When Jesus saw her, he called her forward" (Luke 13:12). Her journey to freedom hinged on her willingness to take the difficult step of responding to the promptings of Jesus. This is one of the most important details in this moving passage. And if you read it quickly, you can miss it altogether. *Jesus called her forward*. No one with a deformity of any kind wants to step up to the public platform. Jesus is calling a deformed woman out of the shadows of her own personal basement into the spotlight. This is a difficult moment, but she responds and takes the first painful step forward. She has to leave the comfort of her hiding place and take the risk of stepping into an uncertain future.

"Woman, you are set free from your infirmity," Jesus clearly says. "Then he put his hands on her, and immediately she straightened up and praised God" (Luke 13:12–13).

This woman's journey to wholeness of body, soul, and spirit began with one bold step forward. Her first step took her out of the shadows and into the vulnerability of her greatest insecurities.

So many of us stop at the entrance to the basement. We remain in the coolness of the underground, putting off our first bold step. We are so close yet remain so far until we take the step. All of us who are stuck have to wrestle with that first important step.

Many people have visions and dreams and live at the edge of their basement. But the hard steps are where we get stuck. As a church, we had to take the hard step of releasing leaders, groups of people, and resources to start new campuses around the city. The first time we launched a group of people to another community, I had to force myself to celebrate on the outside, but I mourned on the inside. I knew it was the right step, but it was difficult to release close friends. We struggled with feeling like we did not have enough leaders, sufficient finances, or enough expertise to move forward. I have never known a person or organization moving into something new that doesn't feel nervous or uncertain about the future.

It always starts with a first bold step.

TIME FOR A BOLD STEP

Over the past decade I have helped lead encounter retreats for both men and women. Hundreds of people attended these weekend retreats each year that focus on walking in freedom. Each year we end the retreat by asking those attending to write down the bold steps they will take once they leave the retreat. Many of them publicly announce their bold step before walking through the "victors lane," where supporters high-five them and shout words of encouragement. I remind each participant that each of us has "a cycle to break, a bold step to take, and a legacy to make." The best bold steps have several things in common.

- They are always difficult to take and usually involve facing a major fear. Let's be honest. If it were easy, you would have taken this step a long time ago.
- They are written down and shared with others. Accountability assures that we will follow through.
- They are concrete. The best bold steps are the ones you know you have taken or have not taken. There is no ambiguity.
- They have an expiration date. If our steps have no deadlines, we will be tempted to procrastinate. We can deceive ourselves into thinking we will eventually follow through while we put things off indefinitely. Remember, delayed obedience is ultimately disobedience.
- They are the first step in a longer journey.

The journey out of the basement is different for everyone but here are some of the steps that I have heard:

I am going to gather my three children and apologize for not being the father God has called me to be.

I am going to propose to the woman I should
have married several years ago.

I am going to call my father and release him
from the bitterness I have held against him for
fifteen years.

I am going to join a twelve-step group and finally
deal with my addiction.

I am going to break up with my boyfriend who is
not a believer and is not God's best for my life.

I am going home to wash my wife's feet and ask
her to forgive me for not being a servant leader.

I am cutting up my credit cards and declaring a
war on debt.

I am taking the step of baptism and boldly stepping into my new life in Christ.

The challenge is not simply to emerge from the basement, but to step out as a changed person. Every new
season requires a fresh sense of purpose accompanied by
renewed vision for the future. What bold step do you
need to take?

CROSSROAD

The time comes when a person needs to say goodbye to the safety of the familiar and launch out into the risky world of the next season. You have a divine assignment. You may not fully understand it or be able to explain it yet, but you can discover it. And you must!

Reading about how to move forward is the easy part. Putting into practice the five steps to moving forward is much more challenging. Let me encourage you to carve out some time for a personal "Moving Forward" mini-retreat. Give yourself time to think, pray, and work through these five steps by yourself. If you can get away, that's even better. Get a notepad and write at the top: My Next Season. Then list each of the five steps with room under each step to write. As you think and pray, ask the Holy Spirit to give you insight to prepare for your next season. Then take time to work through each step, writing down specifically what you need to do about each step.

FIVE STEPS TO MOVING FORWARD

1) Quiet Your Soul to Listen
2) Re-envision Your Life Story

3) Adjust Your Thinking
4) Invite Others to Your Journey
5) Take the First Bold Step

You may be looking with apprehension and uncertainty at what your next season means, but you are beginning to see glimmers of visions and dreams. The possibility of a new season is opening before you. You have the opportunity to make your next season the best season of your life. You have a choice. You can stay in the comfort and relative security of your past, or you can choose to risk again. If you want to live, laugh, love, dream, and pursue your God-given call, then you have but one choice.

It's time.

Take a deep breath. Step out.

ACKNOWLEDGMENTS

Bob and Minnie Jobe, my parents, who left their country and friends to live on mission when I was just six months old. They taught me that life is an exciting adventure worth living for God.

My amazing wife, Dee. She has stood beside me, believed in my calling, and partnered with me in every phase of life and ministry. She laughs with me harder than anyone else I know.

My kids, Marissa, Josiah, and Grant. I am grateful every day that God chose you to be my kids and that you are walking with Jesus.

I appreciate the careful editing and insightful comments of Amy Simpson and the outstanding team at Moody Publishers.

NOTES

Chapter Two: Quiet Your Soul to Listen

1. Henry Cloud, *Boundaries for Leaders: Results, Relationships, and Being Ridiculously in Charge* (New York City: Harper Business, 2013), Kindle.
2. Brother Lawrence, *The Practice of the Presence of God* (Radford, VA: Wilder Publications, 2008), 39–40.

Chapter Three: Re-envision Your Life Story

1. A. W. Tozer, *The Knowledge of the Holy* (1961; repr., New York: HarperOne, 1978), 1.

Chapter Five: Invite Others to Your Journey

1. Robert D. Putnam, *Bowling Alone: The Collapse and Revival of American Community* (New York: Simon & Schuster, 2000), Kindle.
2. This study has often been cited in speeches, blogs, sermons, and other sources and is widely available on the Internet.
3. Wayne Cordeiro, *Leading on Empty: Refilling Your Tank and Renewing Your Passion* (Ada, MI: Bethany House, 2010), 95.
4. That is a finding of a survey by LifeWay Research of 1,000 American Protestant pastors; see "Pastors Feel Privileged and Positive, Though Discouragement Can Come," LifeWay

Research, October 5, 2011, https://lifewayresearch.com/
2011/10/05/pastors-feel-privileged-and-positive-though-
discouragement-can-come/.

5. Henry Cloud, *Boundaries for Leaders: Results, Relationships, and Being Ridiculously in Charge* (New York: Harper Business, 2013), 198–99.

ABOUT
THE AUTHOR

Mark Jobe is an author, radio host, pastor, social entrepreneur, and college president in the city of Chicago. He is the tenth president of the Moody Bible Institute and founding pastor of New Life Community Church, ministering to thousands of people at twenty-eight locations throughout Chicagoland. Dr. Jobe can be heard on his daily teaching program, *Bold Steps*, on stations throughout the country. He is the founder of New Life Centers, a nonprofit focused on mentoring at-risk youth in Chicago. Mark and his wife, Dee, serve as a team together and have three children.

GET THE RESOURCES YOU NEED FOR WHEN LIFE TAKES AN UNEXPECTED TURN.

978-0-8024-2332-0

978-0-8024-2338-2

978-0-8024-2341-2

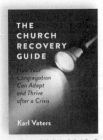

978-0-8024-2343-6

978-0-8024-2344-3

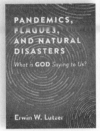

978-0-8024-2345-0

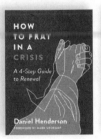

978-0-8024-2359-7

978-0-8024-2360-3

Be it in the midst of a natural disaster, global unrest, or an unforeseen pandemic, the repercussions of unprecedented change can leave us all reeling. Get the wisdom, encouragement, and peace you need to ease your anxieties, strengthen your relationships, and encounter the almighty God during such trying times.

also available as eBooks

MOODY Publishers®

From the Word to Life®